The Life and Work of
Vincent van Gogh

Sean Connolly

www.heinemann.co.uk/library
Visit our website to find out more information about **Heinemann Library** books.

To order:
 Phone 44 (0) 1865 888066
 Send a fax to 44 (0) 1865 314091
Visit the Heinemann Bookshop at www.heinemann.co.uk/library to browse our catalogue and order online.

First published in Great Britain by Heinemann Library,
Halley Court, Jordan Hill, Oxford OX2 8EJ, part of
Harcourt Education.
Heinemann is a registered trademark of Harcourt
Education Ltd.

© Harcourt Education Ltd 1999, 2006
The moral right of the proprietor has been asserted.

Editorial: Clare Lewis
Design: Jo Hinton-Malivoire and Q2A Creative
Illustrations by Sam Thompson
Production: Helen McCreath

Printed and bound in China by South China Printing
Company

10 digit ISBN 0 431 09882 4
13 digit ISBN 978 0 431 09882 1

10 09 08 07 06
10 9 8 7 6 5 4 3 2 1

British Library Cataloguing in Publication Data
Connolly, Sean
The Life and Work of: Vincent van Gogh
759.9'492
A full catalogue record for this book is available from the
British Library.

Acknowledgements
The publishers would like to thank the following for
permission to reproduce photographs:
Page 5, Vincent van Gogh Self Portrait with shaven head,
Credit: The Bridgeman Art Library/Fogg Art Museum. Page
7, Vincent van Gogh Milk jug, Credit: Stichting Kröller-
Müller Museum. Page 8, Portrait Photo of van Gogh's
uncle, founder of The Hague branch of Goupil & Co.,
Credit: AKG. Page 9, Vincent van Gogh Noon, or The
Siesta, after Millet, Credit: The Bridgeman Art Library. Page
10, Coal mining in Belgium, Credit: AKG. Page 11, Vincent
van Gogh Miners' Wives, Credit: The Bridgeman Art Library.
Page 13, Vincent van Gogh Portrait of Theodore van Gogh,
Credit: The Bridgeman Art Library. Page 15, Vincent van
Gogh Two Peasants Planting Potatoes, Credit: The
Bridgeman Art Library. Page 17, Vincent van Gogh The
Allotments, Credit: The Bridgeman Art Library. Page 19,
Vincent van Gogh Portrait of the Artist, Credit: Image
Select. Page 21, Vincent van Gogh The Night Café, Credit:
B & U International. Page 23, Vincent van Gogh Self-
Portrait with bandaged ear, Credit: Exley/Rosenthal. Page
25, Vincent van Gogh The Asylum Garden at Arles, Credit:
The Bridgeman Art Library/Oskar Reinhart Collection. Page
27, Vincent van Gogh Wheatfield with Cypresses, Credit:
AKG. Page 29, Vincent van Gogh Crows over wheatfield,
Credit: Exley/Rosenthal.

Cover photograph: The Dance Hall at Arles by Vincent van
Gogh, reproduced with permission of Bridgeman Art
Library.

The publishers would like to thank Nancy Harris for her
assistance in the preparation of this book.

Every effort has been made to contact copyright holders of
any material reproduced in this book. Any omissions will be
rectified in subsequent printings if notice is given to the
publishers.

The paper used to print this book comes from sustainable
resources.

Some words in the book are bold, **like this**. You can find
out what they mean by looking in the Glossary.

Contents

Who was Vincent van Gogh?

Vincent van Gogh was a Dutch artist. He used paintings to show his strong feelings. He made many great paintings in his short, sad life.

This **self-portrait** shows Vincent aged 35.
This was about two years before he died.
He was very unhappy.

Early years

Vincent van Gogh was born in Holland on
30 March 1853. His father was a **pastor**.
Vincent's younger brother Theo was one of
his few friends.

Vincent was good at drawing. He made this **sketch** when he was nine years old. It shows how well he could draw what he saw around him.

Different jobs

Vincent left school when he was 15 years old. He worked in many different jobs. His uncle got him a job with an **art dealer** in London. This is a photograph of his uncle.

In his job Vincent saw paintings by many great artists. He liked a French artist called Millet. In 1890 Vincent made this painting. It looks like a painting by Millet.

Among the poor

Vincent found his work hard and lost his job. He wanted to make a big change in his life. He began to **study** to be a **preacher.** He studied in a **mining** area of Belgium.

Vincent soon left these studies and went to preach to **miners**. He gave away his things to these poor people. This painting shows some of the miners' wives.

Drawing his feelings

When Vincent was 27 he gave up **preaching** and **studied** art. Then he went to join his family. Vincent's parents had moved to Etten, a small Dutch village.

Vincent argued a lot with his father and other people. Vincent shows his father's serious face in this **sketch**.

Sadness

Things got worse between Vincent and his family. Vincent left home and moved around Holland and Belgium. His father died in 1885. Vincent felt sad.

Vincent felt happier when he was able to draw and paint. He loved showing ordinary people at work.

Moving to Paris

In 1886 Vincent went to Paris to live with
his brother Theo. He saw how a group of artists
called the **Impressionists** worked outside. Their
paintings were full of light and colour.

Vincent also began to work outside. This is a painting of gardens in a village near Paris. Vincent used quick **brush strokes** to make the picture.

Bright colours

Theo helped Vincent meet other artists in Paris. Vincent began to paint with bright colours. The colours showed Vincent's moods and feelings.

Vincent added the bold colours of this **self**-**portrait** quickly and thickly. His face seems to look out through a crust of colours.

Going south

In 1888 Vincent moved to southern France. A painter called Paul Gauguin joined him in the town of Arles. Both artists loved the colourful countryside there.

Everything about the south seemed exciting to Vincent. This lively painting of a café at night shows these feelings.

Signs of trouble

Vincent often became angry or sad. Paul Gauguin left after a quarrel. Vincent felt bad almost all the time. In December 1888 he cut off part of his left ear. He was taken to hospital.

Vincent felt calm again as the ear got better. He began to paint again. This **self-portrait** shows the bandage on his ear.

Illness

The peace did not last long. Vincent began to hear strange voices in his head. In May 1889 he entered a special hospital called an **asylum** to be looked after.

Vincent felt better at the asylum. He painted there. The doctors thought this was a good idea. This painting shows the peaceful garden of the asylum.

Burst of joy

Vincent spent a year in the **asylum**. He painted more than 150 pictures. He sent some to Paris but could not sell them.

Vincent's work was better than ever. The colours and curving lines of this painting seem full of his excitement.

Vincent's last days

Vincent went to live near Paris. He still painted but became sad again. Theo asked a kind doctor to help Vincent. Even the doctor could not cheer him up.

This is one of the last of Vincent's 800 paintings. He was sad and afraid when he painted it. Vincent shot himself on 27 July 1890 and died two days later.

Timeline

1853   Vincent van Gogh is born in Groot-Zundert, Holland on 30 March.

1869–76   Vincent works for the **art dealer** Goupil in Holland, London and Paris.

1877–81   Vincent trains to be a **preacher** and then lives with Belgian **miners**.

1881   Vincent joins his family but quarrels with his father. He travels around Holland and Belgium.

1885   Vincent's father dies.

1886   Vincent goes to live with his brother Theo in Paris.

1888   In December Vincent cuts off part of his ear.

1889   Vincent goes into an **asylum** for a year.

1890   Vincent settles in Auvers-sur-Oise near Paris in May. Vincent shoots himself and dies on 29 July.

Glossary

art dealer person who sells paintings

asylum hospital where people with mental illnesses are looked after

brush strokes marks left by an artist's paint brush

Impressionists group of artists who painted freely, showing light and movement

miner someone who digs for coal underground

mining digging coal from under the ground

pastor someone who leads a local church

preacher person who tells others about God

self-portrait picture an artist makes of himself

sketch another word for a drawing

study learn about a subject

More books to read

Masterpieces: Vincent van Gogh, Shelly Swanson Sateren (Franklin Watts, 2004)

Famous Lives: Vincent van Gogh, Anna Claybourne (Hodder Wayland, 2005)

More paintings to see

Thatched Roofs, Vincent van Gogh, Tate Gallery, London

Farms near Auvers, Vincent van Gogh, Tate Gallery, London

The Oise at Auvers, Vincent van Gogh, Tate Gallery, London

Index